KILLER CREATURES

SNAKE

DAVID JEFFERIS
AND
TONY ALLAN

RAINTREE
STECK-VAUGHN
PUBLISHERS

A Harcourt Company

Austin   New York
www.steck-vaughn.com

Library of Congress Cataloging-in-Publication Data
Allan, Tony.
Snake/Tony Allan and David Jefferis.
p. cm. —(Killer creatures)
ISBN 0-7398-2873-8
1. Snakes—Juvenile literature.
[1. Snakes.] I. Jefferis, David.
II. Title. III. Series.
QL666.O6 A54 2001
597.96—dc21   00-059212

Printed and bound in China
1 2 3 4 5 6 7 8 9 0 03 02 01 00

Acknowledgments
We wish to thank the following individuals and organizations for their help and assistance and for supplying material in their collections: Alpha Archive, Ardea London Ltd., D. Avon, Anthony Bannister, BBC Natural History Unit, Ian Beames, Bruce Coleman Collection, Jane Burton, Alain Compost, Jack Dermid, Michael Doolittle, Xavier Eichaker, FLPA, MPL Fogden, Jeff Foott, CB and DW Frith, Fuji film, E. Hanumantha Rao, Daniel Heuclin, Ken King, S. Krasemann, P. Kumar, Yves Lefevre, Brian Lightfoot, Ken Lucas, Chris Mattison, Mark Mattock, Joe McDonald, NHPA Natural History Photographic Agency, Oxford Scientific Films, Papilio Photographic, Planet Earth Pictures, Hans Reinhard, Jany Sauvanet, Seaphot Ltd., Still Pictures, John Visser, Martin Wendler, Mike Wilkes, Rod Williams, ZSL

▲ A snake flicks its tongue to pick up scents in the air. In the snake's mouth there is a special body organ that lets the snake "taste" the air from scents on the tongue (see page 8).

CONTENTS

LOOK FOR THE SNAKE BOX

Look for the little black snake in boxes like this.
Here you will find extra snake facts, stories,
and other interesting information!

WIGGLY HUNTERS

There are more than 2,600 species of snakes. They come in various sizes—from as long as a truck to shorter than a pencil!

All snakes are hunters, whether they catch worms and grubs or animals as big as goats or deer. Some snakes lie in wait for their prey, while others chase after it. They all strike with lightning speed at the kill.

Snakes are found in most parts of the world, especially in hot countries. There are also about 50 species that live in water. The only places without snakes are a few islands, including Ireland and New Zealand, and very cold regions that are covered with snow and ice.

▲ The reticulated python is a huge snake. The longest ever seen was measured at more than 33 feet (10 m)!

▶ The green tree python from Southeast Asia can grow to nearly 7 feet (2 m) long. Snake skin is usually dry and warm. This surprises some people, who expect it to be cold and slimy.

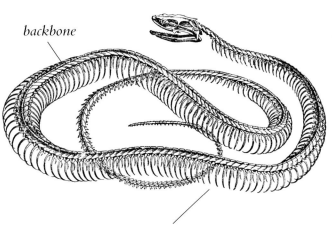

backbone

Count the ribs!

A snake's wiggly skeleton is made up of a backbone and many ribs. A really big snake may have more than 500 pairs of ribs, while humans have just 12 pairs. Inside, the snake's body organs are shaped to fit. Its kidneys, for example, are long and thin. Some snakes have only one lung, instead of the two we have.

The python lies with its head on top of its body, coiled around a branch.

5

MOVING ALONG

Snakes move around very well, considering that they have no arms or legs. They can glide smoothly on land, climb trees, and even go swimming.

Snakes move mostly with an S-shaped serpentine motion. Their body scales grip against bumps in the ground, while the snake uses its muscles to wiggle ahead.

Other snakes move slowly in a straight line, using a "caterpillar" crawl. Their belly scales bunch upward in waves, and the snake pushes forward, like a caterpillar. Big snakes, such as the boa, move like this most of the time. Some burrowing snakes move undeground by pushing against the sides of their earth tunnels.

▲ Most snakes move in an S-shaped motion. The body pushes against bumps in the ground.

▼ A horned viper in the Sahara Desert. Snakes move on loose sand using a "sidewinder" motion. The snake throws its head and body sideways, leaving tracks like rungs in a ladder.

A tree boa can hang safely as long as it has enough coils wrapped around a branch.

▲ South American boas coil around branches. Climbing trees is no problem for snakes. They use their scales to push against bumps in the bark.

SNAKE SENSES

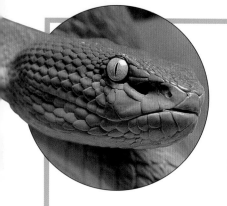

▲ Different kinds of snakes have different skin patterns. But all snake skin is sensitive to heat and touch.

The most important snake senses are smell, taste, and touch. Some snakes also have an extra sense that allows them to track prey in the dark.

Snakes see things in less detail than humans, but they can spot tiny movements. Snakes do not hear well, because they do not have external ears. They do have inner ears, which can detect vibrations, such as the steps of a mouse.

Snakes have a keen sense of smell and can also "taste" the air. A snake flicks its forked tongue to collect scents. These are placed in tiny holes inside the mouth that are linked to the snake's brain.

The snake's tongue tastes the air.

Pits are small openings in the snake's skin.

Three groups of snakes—boas, pythons, and vipers—use an extra sense. They have small holes in their heads that are called pits. These look like extra nostrils but can detect changes in temperature. These snakes can hunt prey in the dark, because they can sense the warmth of an animal's body against the cooler air around it.

▲ This horned viper lives in the Sahara Desert. Pits in front of its eyes detect heat and help the snake hunt in the dark.

◄ A green leaf makes good camouflage for a South American snake. It tastes the scent of nearby prey, which may be the snake's next meal.

✺ FOOLED BY A SMELL

Snakes use their sense of smell to tell them what to eat. The hognosed snake of North America usually eats animals such as toads. Experts carried out tests to prove how important smell is for a snake on the lookout for prey. They treated strips of raw beef so that they smelled more of toad than of beef. When the snake was given the beef, it gulped the meat down!

SNAKES NEED HEAT

Snakes are reptiles, creatures that need heat to be active. This is why there are more snakes in hot countries.

◄ A young grass snake tastes the air on a warm spring morning. This snake lives in cool climates. It is harmless to humans.

In the morning, a snake warms up by lying in the sun. If it gets too hot, the snake moves into the shade. A snake spends its days moving between sun and shade to stay the right temperature.

Toward sunset, snakes seek places that are still warm from the day's heat. At night, snakes slow down, until they fall asleep.

WHAT IS A REPTILE?

Reptiles are cold-blooded animals. They have a backbone and dry skin, which may be made of scales or horny plates. Other reptiles include crocodiles, alligators, and turtles. They all lay eggs. Warm-blooded animals, such as humans, have bodies that stay the same temperature. If it is hot, we sweat to keep cool. In cold weather we use food energy or burn off body fat to stay warm.

Staying warm is easy in sunshine, so most snakes live in hot places. But there are snakes that live in cooler places.

In the autumn a snake seeks a winter den. This may be a burrow or hole in the ground, perhaps a hollow tree—anywhere that shelters the snake from the cold.

As winter comes, the snake's body stiffens, and its heart beat and breathing slow down. The snake falls into a winter sleep, called hibernation. The snake hibernates until spring, when it wiggles out of its den, ready to catch the new year's first meal.

▲ An adder lies on a rock in Scotland. The snake flattens out to catch as much sun as possible. Adders are active only in the summer, because Scotland has cold winters.

BABY SNAKES

Most snakes lay their eggs on dry land. The eggs are usually laid in a hole in the ground, in a gap between rocks, or even in a mound of damp grass.

▲ Hatching time for an eastern hognose snake. When it is an adult, the snake's main food will be toads.

Snake eggs are usually oval-shaped and have a leathery shell. In the egg, a baby snake grows until it is ready to hatch. This takes from one to three months, depending on what kind of snake it is.

Just before a snake hatches, the egg starts to look wrinkled, and you may see cuts on the shell. These are made by the snake's special egg tooth. The snake leaves the egg through one of the holes it has cut.

SHEDDING SKIN

Humans shed bits of dead skin all the time, but snakes lose their old skin in one piece. This process is called molting.

When a snake is about to molt, its skin turns dull, especially around the head. The snake may stop eating and hide for a few days. Then the snake rubs its nose on something rough to loosen the skin. The skin starts to split, and the snake slides out of its old skin.

Young snakes molt several times as they grow up. Adult snakes molt three or four times a year.

▼ A grass snake with her clutch of eggs. They are soft and leathery, unlike bird eggs, which break easily.

The female timber rattlesnake stays with the babies for a few days after birth, to guard them. But this is unusual, and life for a young snake is very dangerous. Frogs, birds, small mammals, and even other snakes all like to have a tasty meal of young snake!

AMAZING JAWS

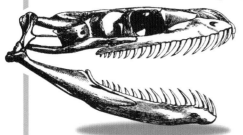

Snakes almost always swallow their prey whole. To do this, they have special jaws that can open amazingly wide.

▲ The python has sharp teeth to seize prey. The back-sloped teeth act like hooks. So it is hard for the animal to escape.

The upper and lower halves of a snake's jaw are joined by stretchy ligaments. This allows a snake to open its jaws wide enough to swallow prey that is much larger than the snake itself. Once the animal is in the snake's stomach, the snake may take days to digest it.

TRAPPED BY THE WIGGLING TAIL

A snake has to catch its prey before it can use those wide-opening jaws. The Australian death adder starts its hunt by setting a cunning trap. The snake lies very still, with only one thing moving, the tip of its tail. The snake wiggles this gently, so that it looks like a juicy worm. When a hungry lizard or other worm-eating creature comes near, the adder strikes.

The skin becomes paper-thin as it stretches around the egg.

The egg-eating snake has a super-stretchy mouth. Five kinds of this small snake live in Africa, and another one lives in India. The snake opens its mouth and slowly works its jaws around the egg. This may take up to half an hour.

Once the egg has been swallowed, it is broken by spines sticking out from the snake's backbone.

▲ Once it has swallowed the yolk and white, the egg-eating snake spits out the crushed shell.

15

THE BIG SQUEEZE

Most snakes eat their prey alive. But some snakes, called constrictors, squeeze their prey to death before they swallow it whole.

▲ Constrictors have little trouble with small prey animals. Here an emerald tree boa eats a mouse only a few minutes after catching it.

Constrictors are the world's biggest snakes. They include the boas of South America and pythons of Africa and Southeast Asia.

A constrictor first bites its prey, then quickly coils around it. The prey is squeezed, not crushed. But this is enough to stop it from breathing. Usually the struggle is over quickly. But with a big animal, such as a crocodile, the fight may go on for hours. After a big meal a constrictor may not need to eat again for a week or more.

▲ Here an anaconda has nearly squeezed a caiman (a type of crocodile) to death. The snake may take an hour or more to swallow this big creature.

▼ Indian rock pythons grow to more than 20 feet (6 m) long.

ROUGH ENDING

The wart snake of Southeast Asia lives on the bottom of rivers and ponds. Its lumpy skin makes it look like a stone or tree branch. When a fish rubs against the wart snake, it coils around the fish and holds on firmly until the prey suffocates.

POISONOUS SNAKES

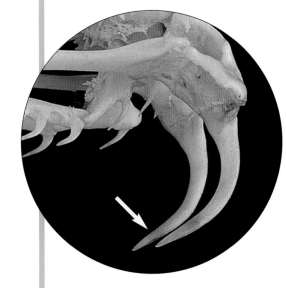

▲ A rattlesnake's skull shows the needle-sharp fangs (arrowed) that inject poison into their prey.

Some snakes kill by poisoning their prey. When the snake bites, the poison, called venom, squirts through hollow fangs.

Only poisonous snakes have fangs. Sometimes the venom is strong enough to kill an animal right away. Sometimes a snake waits for its victim to collapse before moving in to eat.

Vipers are snakes with fangs that fold back inside their mouths. The fangs swing forward when the snake is ready to bite. Cobras and mambas have fixed front fangs. Other snakes squirt venom through short, back teeth.

About one in five kinds of snakes are poisonous to humans. But only a few can kill. The most dangerous snakes include the African black mamba, the Indian cobra, and the Australian tiger snake.

S LIGHTNING BOLT OR SNAKE BITE?

The chances of being seriously harmed by a venomous snake are not very high. Experts think that people in the United States are 15 times more likely to be killed by lightning than they are to die of a snake bite. Even so, if you go walking through the backwoods, it is wise to be careful and wear proper clothes and boots. Anyone who is bitten should seek medical help—quickly.

▲ This gaboon viper lives in West Africa. The snake's fangs grow about 2 inches (5 cm) long—about the same length as your finger.

► The gaboon viper eats all kinds of small animals, including mice. It knocks out its prey with venom before swallowing.

RATTLER!

Rattlesnakes, or "rattlers," bite more people than any other venomous snake in North America.

▲ The pygmy rattlesnake is the smallest rattler. It is just 20 inches (50 cm) long. But it can be as fierce as the much larger diamondback.

The "rattle" that gives the rattlesnake its name is made of pieces of dead scales, left at the tip of the snake's tail when it molts. A piece is added each time the rattlesnake sheds its skin. When a rattler feels threatened, it rears up and shakes its tail. This makes a terrifying buzzing noise as a warning signal. If the signal is missed, the snake may strike with its poisonous fangs.

The rattle is not a reliable warning, though—sometimes a rattler bites first!

LOOK, NO RATTLE!

The small Catalina Island rattlesnake has no rattle, just a small horny button at the end of its tail. Scientists think that it may have lost its rattle over time, since Catalina Island in Mexico, has no large animals to scare away.

Only rattlesnakes have a rattle, but many kinds of snakes twitch their tails when upset.

▶ A diamondback rattlesnake rears up in a threatening position. Its rattle is raised to warn off enemies. The loudest rattles have about eight pieces of scales. But they are delicate and break off easily.

Rattlesnakes eat frogs, toads, lizards, birds, and small mammals. In turn, rattlers are hunted by king snakes, opossums, and large birds, such as eagles and roadrunners.

diamond-shaped markings on the back of a diamondback rattlesnake

HOODED KILLER

There are many kinds of cobras. The king cobra is the largest, while the spitting cobra can spray deadly venom at an enemy's eyes.

▲ The king cobra is the biggest of the cobras. It grows up to 20 feet (6 m) long.

All cobras can rear up and spread a hood to warn or frighten an enemy. The hood is a flap of skin that stretches over movable ribs. A cobra can raise or lower it in a moment. It warns that the snake may strike any second.

Cobras feed mostly on other snakes and large lizards. The king cobra is the longest cobra species, growing up to about 20 feet (6 m). It is shy, though, and avoids humans. It is the only snake that builds a nest for its eggs.

LISTEN TO THE MUSIC

The monocled cobra has "eyespot" marks on the back of its hood. The different cobra species have different marks.

In India, snake charmers play music to make cobras rear up and sway in time to the music. But a cobra cannot hear the music. It really thinks the swaying musician is a threat. The snake opens its hood in warning and follows the charmer's every move. It is ready to strike if attacked.

◄ An Arabian cobra rears up, ready to defend itself. If it feels threatened, it can spray venom through holes at the front of its fangs. The venom is aimed at an enemy's eyes and can leave the attacker blind.

SNAKES AT RISK?

Many people are scared of snakes and think that they all mean trouble, poisonous or not. But usually it is the snakes that are in trouble.

▲ Indian pythons are at risk because the forests and grasslands where they live are being turned into grazing land for cattle.

In some places, snakes are losing their living space. People are turning the wilderness into farmland and destroying forests. Many snakes are killed for their beautiful skins, which are made into shoes, belts, and handbags.

Snakes help to keep down the number of insects and other pests. In some parts of Indonesia, people think it is lucky to have a pit viper living nearby. These snakes avoid humans but eat rats and mice.

Snakes need to be protected. Even dangerous snakes usually avoid people and attack only if they are threatened.

▲ The Asian rat snake is hunted for its skin, which is used to make fashion items, such as wallets and handbags.

SNAKE MEDICINE

There are many reasons for making sure that animal species do not die out. One of the most important reasons for protecting snakes is medical research. Scientists take venom from some poisonous snakes for use in medicines. For example, some chemicals in the cobra's venom are used in painkilling drugs. The water moccasin's venom has a chemical that helps stop bleeding.

▲ The San Francisco garter snake has become so rare that it is now protected by U.S. law.

▲ Australian burrowing snake

SNAKE FACTS

Here are some facts and stories about the world of snakes.

The first snakes

Scientists think that the first snakes developed 135 million years ago. That sounds like a long time, but other reptiles, such as lizards and turtles, have existed for much longer.

Snakes once had legs but have not had them for more than 100 million years. Pythons and boas have kept the remains of their back legs, as two tiny claws on their underbelly.

Desert highways

Every evening snakes look for warm places. In desert areas, the sand cools down quickly after sunset. But a paved road stays warm for hours. So if there is a road, that is where the snakes go!

Nest cleaner

In Texas, screech owls use earthworm-like blind snakes to help clean their nest holes. The owl first catches a snake, then drops it among the nest's messy droppings and remains of old food. The snake eats small insects that are in the nest. This leaves it a healthier spot for the owl and any chicks.

Record egg layer

The puff adder has more babies than any other kind of snake. Experts have recorded a female who layed 157 eggs at one time. Most snakes lay between six and 30 eggs.

◀ Africa's black mamba is the world's fastest snake. It has been timed in short bursts, moving at more than 12 miles per hour (20 kph). That's faster than you can run!

Danger—snakebite!

Almost half the people bitten by venomous snakes feel no bad effects. But if you are bitten, find a doctor fast! A rattlesnake bite made a researcher's arm swell to twice its usual size. He spent four days in a hospital recovering.

Dry fangs

Venomous snakes can control the amount of venom they inject. Many bites are actually "dry" and are given as a warning to the attacker.

Shortest snake

The thread snake is found on only three islands in the West Indies. The tiny creature measures just 4 inches (10 cm).

Freeze—it's a snake!

Standing completely still near a snake sounds like an easy way to be bitten, but small animals often escape this way. Snakes can spot tiny movements, but they see very little detail. If you stand still, you may be "invisible" to the snake. It does not always work, though, and that's the time to run quickly!

Snacking on snails

The main meal for a South American thirst snake is snails. It uses its lower jaw to get them out of their shells.

Hibernating snakes

Snakes normally live alone, but they often share a winter den. Other hibernating animals, such as small lizards, may share the space, too.

▲ This sea snake lives in the ocean around Australia. Many snakes can swim, but sea snakes spend most of their time in water. They look like eels, but eels are fish and can breathe under the water. The snakes have to come to the surface to breathe.

SNAKE WORDS

Here are some technical terms used in this book.

▲ Green markings let the eyelash viper blend in with the jungle.

camouflage
(KAH-meh-flazh)
Colors and patterns used by various animals to help them blend into their surroundings.

cold-blooded
An animal that cannot warm or cool itself is called cold-blooded. Its temperature matches its surroundings. So it has to move in and out of the sun to stay comfortable.

constrictor
(kun-STRIK-tuhr)
A snake that coils around its prey and squeezes until the animal dies from lack of air.

external ear
(ek-STUR-null)
An ear that sticks out of the head. Snakes have no external ears.

fangs
Sharp, hollow teeth, used by some snakes to inject poison into prey.

hatch
When a baby snake is born, as it comes out of the egg.

heat pits
Holes on the head of some poisonous snakes. The pits can sense heat and help a snake to hunt prey, especially at night..

hibernation
(HIGH-burr-nay-shun)
A sleepy state in which some animals pass the winter to avoid the cold, and when there is little food to eat.

hood
Skin behind a cobra's head that opens out to frighten enemies.

kidney
(KID-nee)
A body organ that separates the body's waste from the blood.

ligament
(LI-guh-ment)
Stretchy body tissue that joins bones. Snake jaws can open wide, because the bones are joined with ligaments.

▲ The rattle of a one-year-old rattlesnake

mammal

A warm-blooded animal that feeds its young milk, such as a human, whale, or dog.

molt

In snakes, to cast off a layer of dead skin. New skin grows underneath to replace it.

prey

An animal that is hunted by other animals for food.

rattle

The end of a rattlesnake's tail, made of pieces of old scales.

reptile

A group of cold-blooded animals that includes snakes, lizards, and crocodiles.

reticulated

(ri-TI-kyoo-late-ed)
A word that means "like a net." It describes the skin pattern of the reticulated python.

scales

In snakes, the small, thin plates that make up the skin. Scales are made of horny material that streches when a snake swallows prey.

species

(SPEE-sheez)
A group of living things that can breed among themselves and have young that can also.

venom

(VEH-num)
A poisonous liquid that is injected in prey by biting or sometimes by spitting.

viper

A group of venomous snakes with hinged fangs that fold back neatly when the mouth is closed.

▶ Before molting, a milky fluid separates the layers of old and new skin. Snakes have a clear scale over their eyes. Here the eye looks white, as the fluid comes behind the old, outer skin.

SNAKE PROJECTS

Making a snake file with photographs, notes, and sketches will help you find out more about these amazing creatures.

◀ It's quite easy to take photographs of snakes, at least if they are safe in a tank. Try not to use the flash on your camera, because it may upset the snake.

▲ A simple camera can give good results if you are careful.

The best place to see snakes is in a zoo. There are usually lots of interesting kinds, and they are looked after well.

Collect your facts in a snake file. Take some photographs, and make sketches to add interest. Look for stories about snakes, too. These will give your file a "newsy" look and make it interesting to read.

▶ Label your photos to show snake features.

The anaconda's markings make good camouflage.

AIR CONSTRICTOR

A constrictor snake kills by tightening its coils each time its prey breathes out. The prey cannot take in fresh air, because the snake is squeezing its chest. Soon the victim suffocates for lack of air. Then the snake can eat.

So just how much air do you normally have in your lungs? Try this experiment to find out!

1. You need a bowl of water, an empty plastic bottle (2 liter size is about right), bendy straws to make an air pipe, and a waterproof marker.

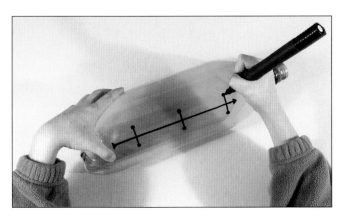

2. Use the marker to draw a measuring line down the side of the bottle. Mark halfway to measure 1 liter, and smaller amounts, too.

3. Join the straws together to make the air pipe. Put one end in the neck of the bottle, ready to blow through the other end.

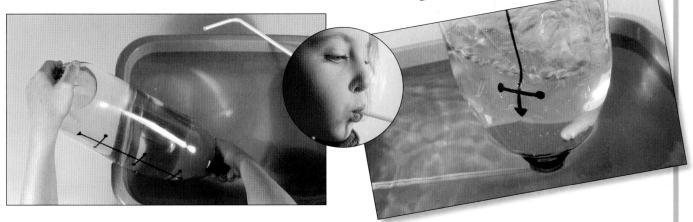

4. Fill the bowl and bottle with water. Then hold your palm firmly over the top of the bottle. Turn the bottle upside-down into the bowl.

5. Blow through the air pipe until you run out of air. Measure how much air you have blown into the bottle. Then have your friends try it.

INDEX